Saint Herman of Alaska

Written and Illustrated by

S. A. Smith

Unexpected Joy Press

Ash Grove, Missouri 2002

Saints For Children Series

Unexpected Joy Press
PO Box 265
Ash Grove, Missouri 65604 USA
417.751.3183
Printed with the blessing of His Grace, Bishop JOB, Archdiocese of Chicago and the Midwest, Orthodox Church in America

ISBN 0-9678400-1-5

Printed in the United States of America

Saint Herman of Alaska

The monk Herman lived alone on an island in Alaska.

He built himself a hut to live in with a place for a fire and a shelf beside it to sleep on.

He found an old cup to drink out of and a cracked saucer to eat from.

He never shaved his beard or cut his hair.

He had many books; some were very old books, some almost worn out from reading.

He wore a deerskin shirt under his cassock. It was a hairy shirt in the beginning, but as it got older, the hair wore off. He wore the same clothes every day.

He wore a heavy cross on a heavy chain under his shirt. That way he would be strong.

He walked all over the island where he lived; many miles some days.

He walked to the ocean and carried back heavy buckets full of seaweed to put on his garden.

He met the people on the island. There were families and children.

Often the fathers and mothers were away and Herman began to teach the children the things they didn't know.

The children loved him and the parents loved to hear him speak.

The people would stay up all night long to hear his wisdom.

Herman could do many things.

He built a small chapel and taught the children how to pray and to celebrate the feasts of the Church.

He built a house for the orphan children to live in and taught them how to live. They called him "Father" because he was good to them.

One boy he called "Gerasim," and Gerasim loved Herman and learned very well all that he was taught.

He walked with the monk through the woods and learned quietness.

He helped Herman in the chapel and learned to pray.

Herman liked to help everyone because he loved everyone.

When anyone was hungry, Herman would catch a fish with his bare hands and cook it and feed the one who was hungry.

If anyone was unhappy or quarreling, Herman would talk to the person and help him or her to see how to improve.

Once there was a danger of water flooding the island. The people came to Herman and asked him for help.

He took an icon of the Mother of God and put it on the ground and prayed. The water continued to rise.

But it never rose higher than the place where Herman had placed the icon.

Herman sometimes walked at night and sometimes he stayed up all night praying and talking with angels.

Herman gathered wood for his fire.

He was so strong from wearing the heavy cross that he could drag huge logs through the woods that no one else could move.

When Herman was quite old, a young woman, Sophia, heard him speaking to the children about loving God, and she asked if she could live near him and learn from him.

Herman refused her, saying he liked to live alone, but she stayed anyway and began to help him teach the children. She taught them to sew and to weave baskets and to plant a garden.

Herman grew potatoes and cabbages and other vegetables, but mostly potatoes, because potatoes grew the best.

Sometimes Herman ate potatoes every day.

Some days he would dry the potatoes on the fireplace and then he would grind them up into powder and mix it with water and make little loaves of potato bread.

Some days he did not eat at all because he would rather pray.

Herman made friends with the animals. His favorite was the bull that lived in the meadow.

He fed the birds pieces of fish.

The ermines, which are not usually friendly to people, were friendly to Herman and lived under his hut. They liked to be with him because he fed them.

He spoke to the bears, asking that they would not harm him,

and they never did.

Herman lived all the rest of his life on the island and never returned to the place where he was born.

He was from Russia and had grown up with monks and Holy Elders.

Sometimes he missed his elders and friends in Russia, and there were times when his heart ached to be with them.

Sometimes angels came to comfort him.

Father Herman stayed at Spruce Island for forty years.

He fed the hungry and healed the sick.

He taught the children the love of God.

People asked him to help them and he always did,

and he still does.

SAINT HERMAN OF ALASKA is a canonized saint of the Russian Orthodox Church. Born in Russia about 1757, Saint Herman began the monastic path at the age of twelve. In 1793, a group of missionaries went out from the Valaam Monastery in Russia to Alaska. Saint Herman was one of these. A church and school were built in Kodiak, and he worked and taught there. Later St. Herman settled on Spruce Island, where he remained for forty years until his repose on December 13, 1837.